GW00692233

TO:

FROM:

A Hip Chick's Guide To Friendship: Words of Inspiration

By CherylAnn Fernandes

Copyright ©2010 by CherylAnn Fernandes
ISBN 978-0-9824493-9-4

Published by Northshire

Illustrated by Daniela Balzano-Fenton
Design by Alison Grieveson

Printed in the USA

A Hip Chick's Guide

to
Friendship

Words of Inspiration

by CherylAnn Fernandes

Illustrations by Daniela Balzano-Fenton

ACKNOWLEDGMENTS

To every soul sister who has touched my life
and made me who I am,
I say thank you.

To Jodi Pshebelski, who I lost touch with after High School and recently rediscovered. How did I last so long without her gentle kindness?

To Ilene Strizver, for all her sage advice, support and encouragement- in everything I do.

To Susan Shaw for giving me a gentle push in getting this book started.

To my design consultant, Alison Grieveson- without her motivation and creativity, this book would have stayed unpublished.

To Daniela Balzano-Fenton, for her many attempts to transform my words into daring and original art, thank you.

To the Goddess Energy that I perpetually ignore and then ask for more clarity and further guidance from. If only I had listened in the first place.

Thanks to you all for being such an integral part of this book.

DEDICATION

To my mother Vera, for being a true Goddess that embodies strength beyond human measure.

To my high school Guidance Counselor, Mrs. June Combs, who believed in, and encouraged me to be myself.

To my best guy-friend Bo Hyatt, who always gives me a true guy's perspective on me.

To Linda Huebner and Elizabeth Clancy. Soul Sisters whose wisdom, compassion and encouragement are unwavering, all the while being a constant reminder of what true friendship really means.

To my friends who I don't often see, speak to or share daily trials and tribulations with, but who I know are always there.

To all the women who have been, are still or will be friends to me. Without your inspirations, influences and insights, these words would not have been created.

PREFACE

This book began with no real idea that it would ever be a book. Words spoken and shared with friends, were just that, words between friends.

It wasn't until I came to realize how much my friends meant to me, how many of them are a part of me, a part of my soul and have made me, well, me.

That's how the idea to somehow share my love for them came about.

I jotted down thoughts, quotes and words wherever I had a spare piece of paper. I had phrases scattered everywhere, with no real idea how to share them with friends. One day, while walking on the beach I knew that my words written should be compiled in a book. And from there, the journey began.

May friends make you a better you!

This book is my gift to you.

Cheryl Ann

TABLE OF CONTENTS

Examining the Unexamined..9

Knowing Them Knowing Me 21

Breakups and Heartaches 33

Accepting without Expecting 39

Empowering and Embracing...49

Examining
the Un-examined

Friends help make
dreams come true

We can lose touch for years,
but when friends re-connect,
we pick up right where we left off

Friends see what we cannot

If I were to travel to a far off land-
never to return-
I would carry my friends-
always
in my heart

Friends are as complex
as the stars
in the universe
and just as plentiful

When I am old,
I hope to have the same old friends
and some younger ones too.
They can push my wheelchair.

Friendships can't be forced-
they just won't work the same

Friends are clairvoyant;
they show up at the
most unexpected times

Friendships just happen!

My friends make me examine
the un-examined me

Hope & Faith
these are the names of a few
of my best friends

In Europe friends saunter down cobble
stone streets,
hold hands, and reminisce,
while in America,
we fear to show such affection.
Why so uptight?

A comfy pillow,
a cushy couch
a good book to lose yourself in
they are just other forms of friends

Being smarter than my friends doesn't work
They would tire of my stupidity

When the hallway is dark,
the doorknob
doesn't turn
and there are no windows to open-
call a friend

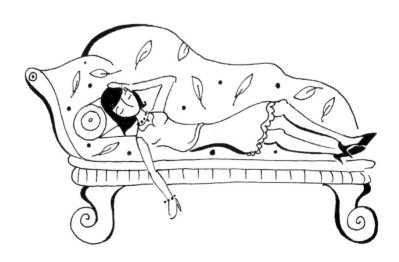

One can be prejudiced
when choosing the keepers of one's
secrets

Use good judgement
when meeting new people
after all,
they might be with you through eternity

My mom was always my friend
I just didn't know it when I was young

Being a loyal friend sure takes a lot of learning;
but I have good teachers-
My friends!

My friends help me dream beyond reason-
but within reality

Silence
between friends
speaks a language
heard by their hearts

Veering off course
and stumbling into friends
is comforting

Friends give me the courage
I would not otherwise have

I challenge my friends to
challenge
ME

When my friend asked me
to be in her will-
   I asked why?
"Because you are the only one
   I trust with my pets",

      she replied.

   Friends take you to the most unexpected places
      and assist in your safe return

Choose your friends with
         thought and care
   They are precious gems

Knowing Them-
Knowing Me

My girlfriends or my animals-
I could never choose
they are interchangeable

Can we survive without friends
Sure.
But why?

If there was a man in my life
who had the same compassion
as my girlfriends-
HE would be the man I marry

An inventory of friends,
old and new
reflects a pattern of consistency,
revealing
I am never without

I once showed up to a social event
dressed exactly
like my girlfriend
If only I would have picked her up,
then she would have had to change.

Wherever I travel,
my friends are still with me
I simply send them postcards

Some of my friends have
    fuzzy little furry paws,
            some aren't so lucky-
        they just have regular ol' hands.

A simple kiss can turn a friend
            into a lover.

For my birthday, my friend
treated me to a workout class.
"Why, I thought.
Why?"

I made a new friend today
she handed me toilet paper
from the next stall.

I liked her shoes.

I liked when my friend gave me clothes
that she no longer wanted-
even though
they were too big for her.

I belong to my friends
because they make me feel welcomed

Similarities bind us
 while differences
 allow us to be individuals
 yet still remain friends

I can be as foolish as I want in front of my dog
                    and she still wants to be my friend

My relationship with me
     can be volatile at times-
       so I ask friends to intervene.

Less than optimal at alone?
Bring a friend along
and lonely disappears

In the spirit of love
        I try to be a good friend
to those
      in need
        of such a simple thing

My friends are my good habits

My dog agrees with me
even when my human friends
don't

Make friends wherever you go
it makes
the journey more enjoyable

Many of my friends have furry
or feathered companions
because of me-
and yes, they are still my friends.

I borrowed a friend once-
never to give her back

Friends
are
my past, present and future

Break-ups
&
Heartaches

After a heartbreak, friends find the pieces
and glue them back together-
with superglue

If my gal pals hadn't been around
after my last break-up,
I'd still be helpless in bed

Friends who emotionally exhaust me
have no place
in my inner circle

A girlfriend who still despises the ex,
after the bitter divorce is long over
and the kids are in college
well, now,
that's a loyal friend-
Heck,
even the dog forgave the ex.

A lost friendship
is like losing
a part of one's spirit.
Eventually,
scar tissue replaces the love
that was once so vibrant.

I giggle
at the ruthless posturing
of faux friends

      then I move on

Friends see things among my chaos,
even though they don't tell me right away-
they wait for the right time,
then hold me until the hurt goes away.

Friends help mend invisible wounds!

I once stayed friends with a woman
because I adored her dog

Friends pick out the shards of doubt
        from my broken heart
and help heal my wounded spirit

During a recent breakup,
 I couldn't bear to see the table set for two,
   the buy one get one specials
      or even a couple holding hands
        so I hid myself in my girlfriend's
          chocolate Angel Food cake

Accepting
without
Expecting

My friends overlook
　　all my imperfections
they think I'm perfect

Straight guy friends dream of undressing me
　　　gay guy friends ask
　　　where I bought my
　　　fabulous shoes

I aspire to be the person
    my friends believe
    I already am

Any friend who let's me borrow her
    sexy black dress and return it
    unwashed, is a true friend

Friends don't care
how lousy you sing
    as long as you are singing

I would find it offensive
if a friend put out the
'guest towels' for me

Girlfriends share intimate details
        within minutes of meeting
Men just stand there
                and hold our coats

I adore my friends foibles,
  It keeps me humble

Friends keep it real-even when
I'm living in pretend

Friends
understand me
often better than
I understand myself

Friends can be seasonal
happen upon us for reasons
or can share our lifetimes.
    Let fate decide

I overlook my friends indiscretions
                    after all,
I am sure they have overlooked mine

Friends know more than
            family ever could or would
                        understand

A woman expects only the best
from her friends
but is satisfied
with whatever they are capable of

How did I earn the friendships I have?
By being a friend back

Aloneness is never for long
when true friends are but
a thought away

I don't ever want to be
without friends
Lots of them

If I sit still long enough
friends show up
in my thoughts

Friends keep the harmony
even when I don't know the rhythm or
the beat

Sometimes old friends don't
　　　　　　　understand the new friends
　　　　　　　but all in all, they are my friends

The prescription to cure life's ills is
　　to be given a dose of 'friend'

Friend dates are the best kind
there are no un-achievable expectations

Even when there is no money
　　　　　　there is always a wealth of friends to buy
me riches

Empowering
&
Embracing

When interviewing for a new BFF
I always ask to meet their pet

Friends bring flowers
when boyfriends don't

The kitchen of a good friend
always has chocolate

Once, I had a friend
offer an old lover to me-
after she was done
of course.

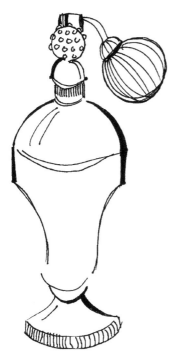

To feel true joy,
share yourself with a
friend

Diamonds aren't a girls best friend
Girlfriends are!

If I can help a friend be
who she wants to be,
than I am a true friend

No matter how much counseling
my friends often force upon me
I still go back

I am selfish with
     my true friendships

Communication
amongst true friends
is often done
while shopping

Freedom to be who
and what you are
is kept sacred by the gate keepers;
Friends!

Honor the Goddess power
of Self
and others will embrace your spirit

A friend who is pushy
or a nag
is only doing it for your own good

An enduring friendship needs
    nothing more than time
to establish its forever presence

Be a friend
        and
            you will always have one

Today's fabulous find while shopping-
a new friend

She said
"don't do it"
and I listened.
Good thing, he wasn't right for me
after all

Settle for nothing less
than true Goddess Power!

Single and its Saturday night?
Find your friends

Actions are inspired
by friends who motivate

Trust your friends
after all
you picked them

Friends give you a chance,
     then another,
          and another after that-
               even when others won't

Friends are the gift
I have been given

A journey with friends
ends up
     being an adventure

Friends don't compete-
they complete

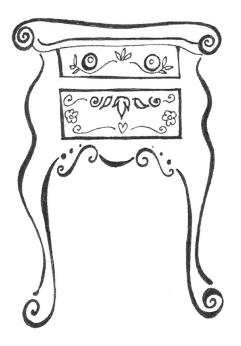

BLESSINGS TO YOU
MY FRIEND.

-CherylAnn

About CherylAnn:

Author CherylAnn Fernandes is a graduate of Duquesne University with a degree in Non Profit Humane Leadership. She works as a Compassion Fatigue Educator and consultant in the field of animal welfare, helping the people who help the animals and dedicates much of her life to homeless and abandoned animals. She writes for a variety of trade magazines, online blogs, is a published poet and short story author.

CherylAnn finds friends to be a source of great strength, loves bargain hunting for fabulous fashion and beauty finds and hasn't met a thrift store she doesn't like.

CherylAnn lives in Milford CT and can be reached at makeup011@yahoo.com.

For more info:
www.AHipChicksGuide.com
www.Facebook.com/AHipChicksGuide